TABLE OF CONTENT

(1)

IGBO

(the name of a language, a people and their god)

The word **IGBO** has been defined by scholars, linguists and historians alike as a name which describes the concept of 'Great Age' (Gbo). In this regard it means 'First People' Ndi Mbu, Ndi Gbo, Ndi Agali Odi in Afa – supposedly understood among Igbo Shaman (dibia Afa) as the ancient Igbo name of the universal language of the First People, now largely lost. The concept of Ndi Gbo is derived from the time-line Mgbe Gbo ('in the Beginning Days of Human History'). Igbo scholars believe that Igbo is derived from Gbo, but our findings are that it is actually the other way round. Gbo is a short form for Igbo and Igbo seems to be one of the earliest words in existence. Yoruba Ifa Mythology says that

'Igbo' is the name of God.

Accordingly, the Yoruba name for 'Almighty God is' Igbo Olodumare. By Ifa definition and mythology, Igbo defines the concept of the 'All Might' and 'All Power of God' – the Creator. The greatest of the sixteen sons and daughters of God who came to re-deem earth from the Evil One, according to Ifa mythology, is a god called Obatala who the Yoruba worship as the ancestor of the Igbos and the greatest of all the Sons of God who have incarnated on earth. They call him 'The Ancient of days' Vice Gerent of the Omnipotent, Mediator between the Almighty and Man. Ifa says he died and resurrected after sixteen days in the grave. And his praise-song says, "Death has no power over Obatala". His title is Obatala Osere Igbo – a title, which according to Ifa, strikes immense fear and awe whenever and wherever it is mentioned, reason being that Igbo is the name of the Almighty in his capacity as the God who dealt an unforgettable defeat upon the forces of evil in the most devastating war ever fought on earth between good and evil. Ifa calls that war "the Great Igbo Battle". This war, needless to say, was the same great battle between good and evil referred to in other great mythologies around the world, not the least of which is the Hebrew Bible.

In Igbo tradition, the word Igbo originated also as the name of a deity. This deity was the father and founder of the Igbo race. Surviving mythology about this entity called Igbo, says he was the founder of the first core Igbo community – a community now called Igbo Ukwu, but which was originally also called IGBO. The ancestor was said to have appeared from nowhere. This was probably during the time of the First People (the cave-men), whom according to ancient traditions of the Egyptians, Igbos and Hebrews, did not die, for in their time death had not yet come into the world. The god-man Igbo surfaced in Igbo Ukwu and taught the cave-men who were then living in Igbo forest-land, the basic arts of survival such as smithing, agriculture and trading. Igbo invented commerce and founded the first market in ancient Nigeria, then known as Nkwo.

Nkwo was actually one of his names – a name which was later corrupted by Europeans into Kwa. European linguists discovered that Igbo, otherwise called Igbo-Nkwo, is the Mother Pot of all cultures in Southern Nigeria, because it is the original culture of the autochthons or cave-men, who themselves were the original dwellers of West Africa and the rest of the African continent. By anglicizing the word Nkwo to Kwa, the early European linguists argued that Kwa was the origin of the Mother Cultures of West Africa which included Ashanti, Akan, Igbo, Yoruba, Benin, Igala, etc. Of late Adiele Afigbo has argued, though not very convincingly that Kwa was a mega-Igbo civilization. But our findings prove him right, for indeed, Kwa mother culture originated from the concept of the 'First People' whom the Igbo and their neighbors called Ndi Ichie Akwu or Akwa Nshi, from which the words Nkwo/Kwa are derived.

In Cross River State the concept of Nkwo is referred to as Qua as well as Akwa Nshi, all of which are expressions of the First People who were death-less and who according to our research findings spoke a divine language known among the native Igbo Shaman as Afa language was the original language of the gods. Today what is left of it is only used by the Dibia Afa during oracular utterances.

(2)
UMUAHIA-IBEKU

Umuahia is the Capital of Abia state located in the middle of the state. Abia state has Umuahia-Ibeku and Aba as its two major cities.

Umuahia was a colonial administrative center for government and Churches. like Methodist, Anglican, Qua Ibo and Faith Terbanacle church.

These Churches set up secondary schools throughout Nigeria and ran them from Umuahia. They owned entities like [1] Methodist collage Uzuakoli, Trinity college, Okwulaga Afara, Women's Teachers Collage Old Umuahia, Women's Teachers Collage Abayi Umuochamu, Queen Elizabeth Hospital umuahia, Ibeku Secondary school, and many more.

Umuahia Ibeku was the Defacto capital of Biafra, where everything settled from Enugu.

Umuahia Ibeku is also the location of

[1] The famous Ojukwu's bunker located in Isisama Afara, home of IPOB leader Maazi Nnamdi kanu.

[2] The Nigeria National War Museum ...where all samples of Biafra war armaments are housed, located at Ugwunchara

[3] The Political capital of abia state...with secretariat in Ndume Ibeku.

The City of Umuahia as it is now made up of Ibeku villages called Amuzukwu to the North,

Afara Ukwu to the south,

Nkata to the North East,

Ohokobe Ndume to South East,

then Osaah and Ugwunchara and Emede Villages to the West.

The name Umuahia started off as a Central Market post called AMA-AHIA meaning market place. But with evolution and bad pronunciations and rewritings...AMA AHIA became UMUAHIA. There have been several legends to tell otherwise but this is it.

But the name Umuahia was not a part of the city name. It was still called Ibeku till the arrival of traders and foreign merchants that brought with them railroad. The Nigerian Government then signed Agreements with IBEKU on the name of the railroad Station to be located in Ibeku. There was a temporary agreement to call the location Umuahia but there was objection. Then the agreement was to have a hyphenated name Umuahia –Ibeku to reflect the owners of the land and domain. Then the name will revert to IBEKU Rail Station. This agreement was to last for no longer than 20 years. The hyphenated Umuahia-Ibeku is still being used till today. There are three railway stations in Umuahia Ibeku.

[1] Amaeke station

[2] Umuahia-Ibeku station

[3] Old Umuahia station.

Umahia Ibeku is located on top of a foot hill that is a part of the Cameroon mountain range that sloped into IMO RIVER. The hills flatten as it passes Ubakala to become one of the even graded paces in the Eastern Part of Nigeria to the edge of Atlantic Ocean at Port Harcourt. This includes all NgwaLand. The city of Umuahia Ibeku has expanded a lot into the surrounded villages and many have found themselves in the middle of the crossroads heading in and out of the city.

This Umuahia ibeku has different names,

Ugwuocha,

ugwu nchara,

ogwumabiri

All referring to the trading post at the center of the city serving all other villages whose market days are to come or have passed in the tradition of buying and selling using market days Afo, Nkwo, Eke, Orie. There are four [4] market days that trades only once a week. Thus they have Afo nta and Afo ukwu, eke ukwu and Eke nta, Nkwo nta and Nkwo ukwu, Orie nta and orie Ukwu. There is always one big market day in a week. This allows the umuahia Ibeku market to serve as a central point for all others for cheaper goods.

There are other big villages that are around Ibeku like Olokoro,

Ubakala,

Old Umuahia,

Umuokpara,

Ohuhu,

Oboro,

Abam,

Item,

Uzuakoli,

Umuahia was an Administrative Center and a big one. Especially during the Regional government era of the 1960's.

Umuahia is the present day capital of Abia State of Nigeria. Was also the second Capital City of Biafra after the fall of Enugu. As the HQ for Bende Division, HQ for Odida Anyanwu areas, Was the Judicial HQ, The HQ for Zone 9 Police Command for all South East Zone before the new police Command at Ukpo.Was also the HQ for both Anglican and Methodist churches of Nigeria where they still have their training collages for their priest called TRINITY COLLAGE in Afara Ibeku.

The HQ of the Assemblies of God mission and their seminary is located at Old Umuahia.

National Root Crops Research Institute in

Amakama olokoro.

The Federal Girls Secondary school in Old Umuahia.

The Federal School of Agriculture at umudike. Government Collage, Umudike-Umuahia,

The Michael Okpara University in Umudike.

Presently, umuahia-Ibeku the Abia State capital territory is made up of two local governments, namely the Umuahia North and umuahia South local government areas.
Umuahia is the home to great people like Dr. Michael Okpara. The former Premier of Eastern Nigeria,
The Supreme Commander of Nigerian Armed Forces.

The President, Maj General Aguiyi Ironsi,

The Governor of Abia State.Gov. Theodore Orji., Finance Minister Dr. Ngozi Okonjo Iwuala, was married to

Umuahia. The NDDC Chairman. Chief Ugochu, Dr JOJ Okezie, Former Fed Minister of Agriculture and Flag bearer for UPGA during Presidential Election. Chief BB Apugo, Chief Ogwulafor, PDP Chairman and Secretary General to PDP, Dr Osisiogu. Former Min of FED Recourses. He has held more ministerial portfolios than any other.

Barrister Ogbonna Director General NIPOST,

Dr Alozie, Head of UNESCO Africa.

Mr. Bob Ogwuagu Special Adviser to several governments,
Brigadier General Emerieh Fed

Commissioner for sports and State Governor. Dr Nwoko
VC UniPort,

Chief Akomas.Mayor Port Harcourt,

Speaker Ohajuruka of Abia state assembly. There are very
many more people but to name a few.

Also in Umuahia you find the famous General Odimegwu
Ojukwu's Bunker used during the civil war of Biafra vs.
Nigeria. In Umuahia you find the first Ceramic industry in
West African and beyond into other countries located in
Umuobia Olokoro, the Golden Guinea Brewery in Afara. The
first Teachers Training Collage ran by the missionaries in
a full scale. The Catholic Church seminary in Ndume Ibeku.
It was in IshiEke ibeku was the first landing place of the
missionaries in Umuahia on their way heading west from
Calabar till they ended up at ONU ICHA [present day
Onitsha]

It was also in Umuahia that the Church encountered the Villagers of Ibeku though the white Missionaries. This was when the famous Okonkwo versus the church called Faith Tabernacle in the village of Ohokobe Afara that left many dead and other out of the area.

(3)

THE UMUAHIA IBEKU WAR

The white men tried to use the faith Tabernacle church in ohokobe to destroy a long standing Igbo Culture when they arrived. They used recruits as missionaries and interpreters of bad deeds in bad faith."

The advent of the white men as the slave masters had their first strong encounter in IGBOLAND particularly at AFARA IBEKU because of this very church, located at Ohokobe Afara Ibeku. This portion of land is between golden Guinea breweries and ceramics industries. When heading out of Umuahia, it is on the left hand side of the road.

How it all started; legend has it that the white men came to IBEKU from Calabar through Isieke Village in Ibeku, their first landing site in Umuahia. This was on their way inland till they got to Niger river. They, the slave masters had with then men who called themselves missionaries spreading a different kind of belief that was strange to the people.

They settled, moved around, recruited people and started preaching their vision of the world to came. While shipping people out of the villages around to far far away lands across the big water called ocean.

They moved around Ibeku then found a place at ohokobe to build their shrine called church. They asked for land and the got the above place and they started building.

When they had a lot of converts, they started challenging the owners of the land. And most of their converts were not from OHOKOBE where the church was being built. There was land encroachments and disagreements.

The white men did not want to settle things but push for a whole takeover of the village. The white men and their recruits abused the ELDERS and CHALLENGED THE RULING

COUNCIL OF THE LAND. The claimed that the ruling group were evil men and will burn in hell because they worship idols. They said that the Elderly men must not be the ruling council but the white men with their recruits that had power over every body. They imposed their condition and made demands and forced contributions from the villagers in other to keep their mission of enslavement going. Forcing people to change their names, separating families as a way to gain control.

This ruling council is/was none other than the OKONKO. It is a secret society

Of wise men of the village. You have to be of age to join. No women allowed.

The OKONKO is the council of wise men of the tribe and elderly men of the village that rule and protected the customs and were/are the custodians of everything natural.

The showdown

The white men and the recruits started arresting villagers and dragged them to their new shrines called church, forcing them to convert and imprisoned them within that confine.

Some elderly members were whisked away to other parts of unknown land, forced them into submission as a way to bring the elders under their control. by imprisonments.

This was not to be. The OKONKO met and decided what was enough of these new found excitement that has cost them their brothers and leaders.

The OKONKO reacted, counter attacked within the whole AFARA CLAN villages of [Isiama, Okwulaga and Ohokobe na umuokeyi]. The reprisal was easy and fast and lasted for days. OKONKO was/is a brotherhood and they fanned those recruits out of all the three villages, not too many escaped the do over search, day after day and night after night. They Killed many of them, burned their houses, any remnant never looked like the original. The church was no more as a congregation. Parts of the building was destroyed. The small completed parts were brought down. Some of the women and Kids that escaped the killings left Ohokobe and the surrounding villages for good to save their lives, especially those who were not originally from Ohokobe. Those recruits from Ohokobe that escaped up till today, the grand children of recruits from ohokobe who escaped have not returned to ohokobe. Rumor has it where most of them are still residing in various parts of

Igbo land. They cannot come back because their lands were given away long time ago and relatives disowned them because of the abomination against OKONKO just to please white men. Those who help protect the recruits were latter kicked out of the villages and acted against.

The white men never came back, they left and that building was left unattended for over 100 years. Generation died with no body to claim ownership of this CHURCH TILL DATE for fear of being linked to the original members. After the war, it still stood unattended. But owners of the lands nearby are now farming around it. Some people set up a nearby church called FAITH but claimed no link to the original Faith Tabernacle. The land stretched out to the main road.

Some people long time ago tried to see is they could form a group to complete the building and take it over but with no success. They just cannot seem to get members.

Now in the front to the right, closer to the main road is a new age church preaching fire and brimstone with holy ghost fire heard out of it.

This is the story about the OKONKO WAR with the Christian White men and their first encounter in

IGBOLAND. There were many more where they succeeded in destroying things. But they lost this one.

This building is still standing, it is a GOTHIC in design, it is a free standing structure with the side wall bearing all the loads from the roof. there is no wooden frame ..all molded frame around the doors and windows.... This building took war bullets at artillery armor shelling with only dents as scratches. It looks like something put up yesterday. look at this picture. Unbelievable. It is stronger than these new structures. It has gone many decades with no roofs on it. Someone has just put some Zink at the back as I can see from this picture.

There was a big orchard around it with fruits that were free for all but nobody wanted to be seen harvesting anything from those trees.

(4)

THE ECONOMIC BLITZ OF   EASTERN NIGERIA

No one conversant with the history of Nigeria in the 1950s and 1960's will miss the overwhelming impact of Dr MI. Okpara on the nation.

After all by 1964 he was fully in charge of the fastest growing and industrializing economy in the world- the Eastern Nigerian economy.

Nothing illustrates the warped sense of history and the complete abandonment of the values of merit and excellence in our national affairs as this willful omission.

The period of Okpara's stewardship of Eastern Nigeria is truly the golden age of Nigerian development.

By 1964- five years after Okpara's ascendancy to the premiership- Eastern Nigeria as recorded by a research group in Michigan State University in the US, Eastern Nigeria was the fastest growing and industrializing economy in the world – ahead of Malaysia, Korea, Taiwan and Singapore.

How did this happen?

It was the culmination of Okpara's unique vision in which agriculture and industrial development were the twin pillars on which he built the Eastern Nigerian economy.

In agriculture his plans had a two-fold thrust- the development of the farm settlements as the anchor for food crop (such as rice) and poultry development, as well as the establishment of estates of oil palm, cocoa, cashew etc. which were processed for export.

Alongside the agricultural projects, were numerous industrial projects scattered over the length and breadth of Eastern Nigeria.

In one frenetic burst of energy, a wave of maniacal and frenzied activity was on-going all over Eastern Nigeria.

As the book reminds us "by January 25, 1963, the Michelin Factory at Port Harcourt was opened. The tire factory was a USD 3,000,000 undertaking.

On March 22, the headquarters building of the Universal Insurance Company was opened in Enugu.

On May 10 the Nigeria Gas factory was commissioned at Emene near Enugu.

On May 16, the Aluminiun Factory at Port Harcourt was opened.

On August 24, the Glass factory became operative in Port Harcourt.

On October 18, the Asbestos Cement Factory was opened in Emene.

On November 9, the foundation of the Central Bank was laid in Port Harcourt.

On November 30, the Golden Guinea Breweries was commissioned at Umuahia, for the production of larger beer and allied products.

On December 13 Hotel Presidential was opened at a whopping cost of BPS £2,000,000.

The burning fire for industrialization led to the establishment of the modern ceramic industry in Umuahia, textile mills at Aba and Onitsha and a shoe factory in Owerri.

There was a catalogue of numerous small industries that were also established simultaneously with the major ones during this period.

It was during this period that the first phase of the farm settlements scheme was established Ulonna in Umuahia province, Ohaji in Owerri Province- Igbariam in Onitsha province, Boki in Ogoja province, Uzo Uwanni in Enugu province, Abak in Annang province.

Each was to accommodate over 5,000 farmers and what was remarkable was the scrupulous effort for even spread of the settlements throughout the length and breadth of the region.

All these activities had been elaborated in his vision for the development of the region after the general elections of 1961.

As he stated..." the period immediately following the elections was a period for building the economic consciousness of the people"

It is this consciousness and burning desire to raise the standard of living of our people, the unflinching determination to assault poverty from all fronts, that has been distilled into the 1962-68 development plan.

Inviting the people as citizens of a democratic region to examine, approve, criticize or condemn any portion of the plan (the plan is the peoples plan) it provides for the development of the small village, it touches on the requirements of the largest city; it caters for the need of the smallest peasant industry and prescribes the means for the mounting of the biggest industries..."

What was remarkable in his vision was the appreciation of the role of the private sector. As he observed to achieve rapid economic growth and raise the standard of living of the people, it was necessary that "the private citizens, the ordinary men and women everywhere must participate by taking a fair and equitable share in our development and industrial projects..."

He elaborates on this vision when he states
".... In encouraging and participating in the industries established in the Region, our government was doing so on behalf of the citizens of the Region. It was, as it were,

holding its shares on trust for the people. As and when the industries have overcome their teething problems and the risk of failures minimized, government proposes to divest itself of most of its shares and the money realized used in pioneering into new industrial projects..."

Thus, the visionary did not only recognize the role of the government as the steward on behalf of the people but more importantly acknowledged the government's fiduciary responsibility.

It was an incredible display of courage in the midst of rampaging risk factors and the energy to pursue long-term goals on behalf of the people.

It was a remarkable demonstration of transparency and accountability. It was a vision that was forty years ahead of its time.

These latter values were illustrated by his commitment to participatory democracy as shown in the fact that he inaugurated an annual series of leaders of thought conferences (a total of five in 1960,

1962, 1963 and 1965).

A remarkable aspect of his industrialization plan was the collaboration and cooperation with foreign investors to undertake the large industries such as Michelin Tyre factory in Port Harcourt and the Nkalagu Cement factory in present day Ebonyi state.

Indeed, in Okpara's long term vision as he told me in a conversation in his home in Nkwoegwu in 1983 was that Port Harcourt through Aba and Umuahia going on to Enugu would have developed into a globally significant industrial mega polis and conurbation.

This drove his passion for the development of the University of Nigeria for which he has not, in my view, been given adequate credit. He provided the money through his prudent management of the resources of the region.

If the politics of those times had been better managed, Eastern Nigeria would have been ahead of South Korea, Taiwan and Singapore for we were indeed ahead of these success stories of the second half of the 20th century.

What was most remarkable was his spirit characterized by his disarming humility and rock-solid determination to confront all the odds frontally. These were exemplified by his return to medical school after the war!

We cannot end this without recognizing the unique strategies he adopted for the management of the government and the instruments he adopted for his far reaching economic programs.

For the latter, the Eastern Nigeria Development Corporation was the engine room for the pursuit of his economic development plans. His management of men and resources was imaginative, innovative and revolutionary.

The most remarkable attribute is that after his stint as Premier of Eastern Nigeria he returned to live in

his father's modest bungalow even as some members of his cabinet had vast estates in their hometown and elsewhere. That speaks volumes of his integrity.

He had arrow heads who coordinated the activities of the government in addition to the informal agencies of democratic participation.

He ceded the day to day running of the party to his old friend Dr L C Mbanugo, the civil service to Sam Oti, the intelligentsia to Professor Kalu Ezera and the economic domain to Odumegwu Ojukwu Snr.

These were his kitchen cabinet at it were and beyond the formal structures of the party and the bureaucracy. Thus, he could exercise an inspiring overview to the business of governance through the formal structures of governance, even as he recognized the validity of the informal networks that are the eyes and could invigorate governance.

In the final analysis his success ultimately rested on his understanding of his people and the operative environment that had shaped him and his people.

He certainly deserves intense study if we are ever going to appreciate where the rain started to beat us given our present circumstances.

The book is an honest effort but is riddled with avoidable typographical and other errors but it is a treasure trove of information on the Okpara years and a wistful reminder of what Nigeria could have been.

Nevertheless, the vision must survive and endure.

(5)
BEFORE THE OIL

At 39 years, Michael Okpara was the youngest Premier of Nigeria & the Eastern Region for six years &

Igweocha know as Port Harcourt was part of the Eastern region. He was responsible for setting up the

Trans Amadi Industrial Area, Hotel Presidential in Igweocha Today's Port Harcourt and Enugu Michelin Tyre Factory in Port Harcourt, Obudu Cattle Ranch in Calabar, the Owerri shoe Industry, the Aba Textile Mill and Port Harcourt sea port expansion.

He did all these with No Crude Oil revenue, but resources from palm oil, coal and limestone.

In Igweocha today's Port Harcourt, Dr. Michael Okpara's visionary acumen blossomed in the establishment and development of a vast Trans Amadi Industrial Estate which, to this day, remains the heart beat and bulwark of industrial development in Port Harcourt, Rivers State.

Dr. Okpara was the son of a laborers but rose to become a medical doctor of distinction. He never owned a house. He practiced "Pragmatic Socialism" and his hobby was building infrastructure development for the Old Eastern Nigeria as well as encouraging agriculture.

After the unfortunate civil war, he went to exile in Ireland where he practiced Medicine. Before his return from exile in 1979, his friends took up the task to build him a house in his village at Umuegwu in Umuahia, Abia state and that was the only house and property he had.

Dr. Michael Okpara died on December 17, 1984 and today, a University of Agriculture is named after him in Umudike and likewise, a street is named after him in Abuja. It was in the house built by his friends that he was buried.

(6)

THE PRESBYTERIAN CHURCH OF BIAFRA (1858)

In April 1846, at the invitation of the two kings of Calabar, a team of missionaries from the Church of Scotland Mission, led by Rev. Hope Masterton Waddell, arrived Calabar where they set up the first congregation of what is now known as The Presbyterian Church of Nigeria. From Calabar, the Church began to grow. In 1858, it was constituted as the Presbytery of Biafra. This Presbytery of Biafra metamorphosed into the The Presbyterian Synod of Biafra in 1921. The Church continued to witness remarkable growth until 1945, when the Presbyterian Church of Biafra was constituted, with the Synod as its highest court. In the same year, the white missionaries handed over the Church administration to Nigerians. The Presbyterian Church of Biafra became the Presbyterian Church of Eastern Nigeria in 1952. By 16th June, 1960, the Mission Church integration was completed and the Church changed its name to the Presbyterian Church of Nigeria. In 1985, the Synods met in Afikpo and agreed to create Regional Synods with the General Assembly as the highest decision making body. This decision materialized on the 22nd August, 1987, when the General Assembly was inaugurated at the Duke Town Presbyterian Church, Calabar. After the creation of the General Assembly, two regional Synods were created in 1988. These were the East and the South-East Synods. As at today, the Presbyterian Church of Nigeria has nine Regional Synods.

The Presbyterian Church of Nigeria is a part of the Holy Catholic or Universal Church. It is one of the results of the Protestant Reformation that was begun in 1517 AD. It worships one God Almighty in the Trinity of the Father, the Son and the Holy Spirit. It rejoices in the sovereign grace of God towards humanity and creation and confesses our Lord Jesus Christ as the eternal Son of God who was crucified for the salvation of humankind and who is the Head of the Universal Church. It believes in the Word of God as contained in the scriptures of the Old and New Testaments as its supreme rule of faith and life. The Church proclaims the gospel of the kingdom of God and invites all to receive the forgiveness of sins and the acceptance by God through faith in Jesus Christ and the gift of eternal life.

From its humble beginning in Calabar in 1846, the Church has been firmly established in Nigeria with congregations spread across the country. The Church has nine Regional Synods, over fifty Presbyteries and more than two thousand parishes, congregations, outreaches and mission fields spread across the entire country. It also has a Mission Presbytery covering the Republics of Benin and Togo. The Regional Synods are those of Akwa (covering Akwa Ibom State, with office in Uyo); Calabar

(parts of Cross River State, with office in Calabar); East (parts of Abia State, with office in Ohafia); East Central (Enugu and Anambra States as well as parts of Ebonyi State, with office in Abakaliki); Mid East (parts of Ebonyi State with office in Afikpo); North (covering the Northern States of Nigeria, with office in Abuja); South Central (Rivers, Bayelsa and Imo States as well as parts of Abia State, with office in Aba); Upper Cross River (covering parts of Cross River State, with office in Ugep) and West (covering Lagos, Ogun, Ondo, Ekiti, Osun, Edo and Delta States as well as the Mission Presbytery of Cotonou/Lome, with office in Yaba, Lagos).

STRUCTURE: The Presbyterian Church of Nigeria, like other Presbyterian Churches in the world, is ruled by Elders. These are classified into two - the Teaching Elders (ordained clergy) and the Ruling Elders. Both the Teaching and Ruling Elders come together to constitute the 'courts' of the Church through which they govern the Church. The Presbyterian Church of Nigerian has four courts - the Kirk Session, the Presbytery, the Synod and the General Assembly. b) Polity: The government of the Church is Presbyterian – a system of governance in which the Elders rule, based on democratic principles. The government is exercised through a court system, as stated above. The courts are the following: i) Session: The Session consists of a Minister (or Ministers) and Ruling Elders who exercise rule under

Jesus Christ in all matters affecting the spiritual well-being and order of the Congregation/s. ii) Presbytery: The Presbytery is made up of the Ministers and the representative Elders of the Sessions that constitute the Court as determined by the Synod. It exercises oversight and rule over the Ministers (including those on probation) and Students for the ministry as well as the Sessions and Congregations within its bound. iii) Synod: This Court consists of all the members of Presbyteries together with such representatives of local interests of the Church as may be authorized by the General Assembly. The Synod acts as an Appeal Court over the Presbyteries within its bounds and also considers matters of local concern to the Church. iv) General Assembly: The General Assembly is the Supreme Court of the Church. In all matters that concern the Church, its decisions are final. It exercises oversight and rule over the Sessions, Presbyteries, and Synods as well as the Church as a whole.

Since its advent in Nigeria, the Presbyterian Church has been vigorously involved in evangelism and social action in fulfillment of its divine obligations. a. Evangelism: From its humble beginning in Calabar in 1846, the Church has been firmly established in Nigeria with parishes spread across the country. Congregations and parishes have been established in all parts of the country and a Mission Presbytery set up even as far as Cotonou and Lome covering the Republics of Benin and Togo respectively. b. Education: Over the years, the Church has been involved in the education sub-sector through the numerous primary and post-primary schools established and run by Parishes,

Presbyteries and Synods. It is interesting to note that in 1895, the Church founded one of the foremost educational institutions in Nigeria - the Hope Waddell Training Institution, Calabar. The institution has since been in the fore-front of producing the educated elites of this country, the number of which includes such names as the first President of Nigeria, Dr. Nnamdi Azikiwe and the first Governor of Eastern Nigeria, Dr. Akanu Ibiam. In furtherance of its commitment to the education sub-sector, the

Church has established a degree-awarding institution - the Presbyterian Health Institute, Uburu, Ebonyi State. The Institute, which is affiliated to the Ebonyi State University, Abakaliki, in the award of degrees in Nursing and related disciplines, is an arm of the Pres byterian Joint Hospital (PJH), Uburu. In addition to the Institute, the Church runs two degree-awarding Theological Institutions - Hugh Goldie Lay Theological Training Institution, Arochukwu, Abia State (founded in 1918) and the Essien Ukpabio Presbyterian Theological College, Itu, Akwa Ibom State (1994). c. Health/Agriculture: Health programs are veritable tools in the hand of the Church for salvation. The Church, under a deliberate policy to care for the body as

well as the soul, has over the years established and run
hospitals and health centers in parts of the country.
These include: -Mary Slessor Joint Hospital (MSJH), Itu,
Akwa Ibom State. -Eja Memorial Joint Hospital (EMJH),
Itigidi, Cross River State. -Presbyterian Tuberculosis and
Leprosy Hospital (PTBLHM), Mbembe, Obubra, Cross River
State. -Urban Health Services (UHS), Aba, Abia State. -
Presbyterian Mission Hospital (PMH), Ivenger, Benue
State. -Rural Improvement

Mission (RIM), Ikwo, Ebonyi State. -The Presbyterian Joint
Hospital (PJH), Uburu, Ebonyi State. -Ekoli Presbyterian
Joint Hospital (EPJH), Ekoli-Edda, Ebonyi State. The
involvement of the Church in the agricultural sub-sector
is also worthy of note. Of particular mention in this area
are the Itu and Yakurr Farms. d. Social Action (PCS & D):
The Church believes that the vehicle through which it
reaches the people with the gospel of Jesus Christ
includes social action – a programme of assisting the
needy in the larger society anchored on the philosophy
that physical and material well -being prepares the
ground for spiritual development. It has therefore set up
the Presbyterian Community Services and Development
Department (PCS & D), for the purpose of assisting the

needy in the larger society. The PCS & D was established to articulate the social-action policy and programs of the Church in the areas of HIV-AIDS prevention and care, emergency relief, women empowerment, justice and peace, destitute rehabilitation, agriculture and adult literacy. It is a fully established Faith-Based Organization, funded by the PCN, overseas Partner-Churches and international donor agencies such as the United States Agency for International Development (USAID). The work of the department is carried out under seven distinct sub-departments namely: i) PRESBY AIDS: As the name implies, PRESBY AIDS was set up to educate Church members as well as the public on HIV-AIDS prevention and care and other related services. ii) Emergency Relief: To cater to the immediate needs of those who have been displaced by any form of disaster by assisting them with food, clothing, shelter and cash as the case may be. iii) Women Empowerment: To empower women to participate fully in politics, economic and other human activities at all levels through education and mass mobilization. iv) Justice & Peace: To engage in Conflict Resolution and facilitative mediation among warring communities or individuals in conflict, and, to fight human rights abuses.

e.g. obnoxious customs and practices against widows. v)
Destitute Rehabilitation: To rehabilitate destitute through
training in various skills and providing micro-credit to
establish cottage industries of their own, and, to facilitate
scholarship for children of destitute who are able to go to
school. vi) Hunger and Food: To train people in modern
agricultural techniques and provide farming input such as
crops, fertilizer and improved seed and animal varieties.
vii) Adult Literacy: Adults who have no formal education
are provided with access to acquiring knowledge and
formal education.

The Presbyterian Church is a first generation Church with
a wide circle of ecumenical relations. It is a member of
the World Council of Churches, Reformed Ecumenical
Council, World Alliance of Reformed Churches, Christian
Council of Nigeria, Reformed Ecumenical Council of
Nigeria and the Christian Association of Nigeria, among
others.

The Church encourages its members and indeed
Christians to be engaged in partisan politics but it does
preach the practice of "politics of righteousness." It is
only when Christians practice politics according to the

teachings of Jesus Christ that we can establish a godly society.

Courtesy of the Directorate of Information & Public Affairs, G. A. Office, The Presbyterian Church of Nigeria, Aba.

(7)

IRI-JI OHUO (NEW YAM FESTIVAL) IN IGBO LAND

Iri-ji festival is one of the popular feast in Igbo, in which

Uturu is among. It is usually celebrated yearly in the month of September in Uturu unlike Mbaise people and many other communities in Igbo land that do celebrate theirs in the month of August. The festival is as old as the community itself.

When yam was first discovered in Uturu, people were eager to take it as food because of hunger but they were at the same time afraid of death, since they didn't know if it would be edible. Achara People, being the eldest lineage in Uturu, were asked to taste the yam. According history, Achara because of fear of death, in turn shifted the risk of tasting the yam to Onuzo, the smallest and the least in Achara. Onuzo People, according to information, obediently took the risk of testing the yam. The whole community waited for two weeks (eight market days) to know if they will die. But finally Onuzo people survived the risk- they did not die. Then other communities joined them.

Today, however, Uturu Community is still giving the Onuzo People that respect, hence they are the first and the only clan (out of the thirty-nine (39) sub-lineages/Clans in Uturu Community) that will harvest and display the New Yam (Ji ohuo) in Nkwo-Achara, the biggest Market in Uturu, before the Uturu New Yam Festival. It is against Omelala, the tradition of Uturu People till date for any Clan, Village or Kindred to harvest or display the New Yam (Ji ohuo) on/before the day of Iri-ji Nde Onuzo in Uturu which comes eight days before the Uturu New Yam Festival.

In the past, the Uturu Iri- Ji festival, like every other part in Igboland, used to go with some sacrifices to appease the god of yam "Njoku-ji", for a good harvest. The farmer after the yam ritual in the farm, will come back home and slaughter a cock (Okeokpa) in front of his Njoku Shrine. He will also pour libation with palm wine and kolanut. The cock will be used to prepare yam porridge "Eweghi", which is only meant for all the male children in the family.

But today, the story is no more, Christianity has rose, tackled and stippled Uturu society some of the negative conditions and practices of her culture and religion. Today with Christianity in Uturu, we no longer talk of "Njoku Shrine and the appeasement of the god of Yam- Njoku Ji, eke igba nsi" etc. as it used to be in the past. A lot of social changes in the cultural and religious practices in Uturu have been recorded. Committed Uturu Christians embrace the Christian faith to the utter neglect of the negative Uturu culture. Without doubt, Uturu is witnessing a social change. In

his theory of social change, Murdock has the view that cultural changes occurs whenever social behavior persistently deviates
from established cultural habits in any direction, it results in modification first in social expectation and then in customs, beliefs and rules. This is indeed the case in Uturu today.

During the period of iri ji, comes ụmụ ụmụ festival.

Ụmụụmụ festival, was or/and is one of the most important festivals in Uturu. It is the day an Uturu Man/Woman receives and hosts a feast with his/her grandchildren, relations or descendants. Umu-umu festival is usually celebrated in Aho/Afo, two days after the Uturu Iri-ji festival. The feast, is only restricted to relatives, descendants and grandchildren unlike Uturu Ibo-ahia festival which is associated with making friends and associates. Umu-Umu in Uturu is so important to the extent that, on that day, even the elders still visit their maternal home.

Although, today the story is no longer the same as Umu-umu has become a story of the past, and the youths are directly or indirectly suffering its negative effect in many areas of life. For instance, some time ago in 2013, a young man from Achara a lineage in Uturu engaged himself in a secret serious relationship with a young girl from Akpukpa another lineage in Uturu which lasted for about 3-4 years before they agreed to marry each other. But sadly their parents stop the marriage, because they are from one descendant. plus, many other examples which we cannot state here because of time and space.

Apart from the joy that goes with the feast, Umu-Umu festival, however, helps one to recount his/her descendants (Umumu). It also helps in the area of marriage or relationship as it was and it is still regarded as an abomination for an Uturu man or woman to marry or have sexual contact with his/her blood relation below his/her fifth generation.

Umu-umu iri-ji festival is as old as the community itself. As I admin witness it till 1998, as we are going to visit our maternal Parents, we go along side with some items like; fowls head, the jaw etc. Me as a first son hands over the head of the fowl to the eldest brother of my mother, while the second son hands over the jaw to my maternal parents. As we are going back, the following items, such as tubes of yam, farm products such as garden eggs;

fluted pumpkin, pumpkin leaves, mushroom etc. will be given to us as gifts from our maternal parents.

None have associates Umu-umu festival with diabolic activities. , As there is no fetish activity attached to the feast going by its tradition(like; Children visiting their maternal parents with fowl's head, the jaw etc)

However way one may look at it, the festival calls for a serious attention. It therefore needs a total religious re-visitation. if there is any Uturu Cultural feast or festival that ought to be modernized so that It can sooth the life and activity of the modern man, I think it should be Umu-umu festival. Our ultimate objective should be to bring back the spirit of Ikwu n'ibe thereby putting into control, our relationship with one another.

(8)

IGBO LESSON

Do you know how to use "na" in Igbo?

Obi na Aba (Obi and Aba)

Obi na-aba (Obi is living)

O bi n'Aba (He lives in Aba)

The word "na" can be used in three ways in Igbo:

1. As a conjunction "and". It must stand alone with no hyphen or apostrophe. Example:

Elu na ala (up and down).

Mmadụ na mmụọ (Human and spirit)

2. As a verb "is" to show continuous tense. It must be hyphenated. Example:

Ọ na-abịa (She is coming).

Ọ na-eme mkpọtụ (He is making a noise).

Ada na-achị ọchị (Ada is laughing).

3. As a preposition. (A preposition shows a location). If the word that comes after the prepositionstarts with a vowel, then an apostrophe will be used to shorten the "na" to "n'."

Examples

O bi n'Enugu. (He lives in Enugu).

Ọ dị m n'obi. (She is in my heart).

But if the word that comes after the preposition starts with a consonant, the "na "must be written in full with no apostrophe.

Example

O bi na Uturu (He lives in Uturu).

Ihe banyere na ntị m. (Something went into my ear).

Igbo is an organized language. You don't just write whatever you like. There are simple rules to make it easy for the reader to understand you. But Igbo is simple to write. You write whatever you say and separate the words the way they are separated in English and observe some simple rules.

Ka anyị na-asụ Igbo na edekwa Igbo. Daalu nụ, Ụmụ Igbo ndị Chukwu gọziri."

(9)

THE IGBO SPEAKING COMMUNITIES IN KOGI STATE

While much is known about the Igbo-speaking communities outside the South-East, but very little is known about the Igbo-speaking communities in Kogi state especially in Ibaji and Igalamela/Odolu LGAs such as the Eke Avurugo community (which speaks Igbo as first language and Igala as second language.

One could find a handful of communities which strongly seem to be Igbo communities going by their names, despite the similarities between Igbo and Ibaji Igala names/words, Ugwuebonyi, Ebokwe, Ozara, Amaeke, Amankpo, Amauwani camp, Amaokwu, Amadiefioha, Amaufulu, etc. all in

Igalamela/Odolu LGA. The Odolu community in Igalamela/Odolu LGA is said to speak Igala as first language and the Nsukka Igbo dialect as second language. In Ibaji LGA, we can see some town names such as Nwajala, Umuoye, Ubulie-Umueze which are, most definitely, Igbo community names. One obvious distinguishing factor between Igbo language and Igala is the lack of 'z' in Igala alphabet which is present in Igbo, which possibly rules out an Igala origin for some towns such as Ozara, Umueze etc.

Akpanya is an Igbo-speaking community located deep in the heartland of Igala land. Very little is known about this town. About 95% of the people speak Igbo/are Igbo natives. The town also houses majority of Igbo Muslims from Igboland.

Igalaland uses the 4 native Igbo calendar days of Eke, Oye, Afor and Nkwo which are Eke, Ede, Afor and Ukwor in Igala land.

(10)

OJUKWU (as a youth)

Biafran warlord, Chukwuemeka Odumegwu Ojukwu and his aunty, Winifred Ojukwu, shortly after he returned to Nigeria in 1955 on completing his studies at Oxford university. Ojukwu bagged a Degree in History.

Ojukwu attended Kings College Lagos, Epsom College, Surrey, England and the prestigious Oxford University, England.

By the time Ojukwu returned to Nigeria in 1955, his father had become one of the richest businessmen in the country with a business empire that spanned Transportation, Banking, Retail, Construction and Manufacturing.

Ojukwu's father took him to his corporate headquarters and showed him a well furnished

air-conditioned office, offering him a top position in his business organization. Ojukwu turned his father down, telling him he wanted to make his own way in life. Ojukwu eventually secured a job in the civil service as an assistant district officer of Udi division, just outside Enugu. In 1956, Ojukwu was posted to Aba. It was at Aba that Ojukwu attended a party that would change the course of his life. At this party, Ojukwu met a young Yoruba man called Adeyinka Adebayo, who had just been newly commissioned as an officer of the Nigerian Army. Adebayo told Ojukwu that the Army was in the process of being indigenized and there was a shortage of officers. A few weeks after this party, Ojukwu was promoted to District Officer and posted to Calabar.

On hearing that his son had been posted to Calabar, Ojukwus influential father prevailed on the authorities to cancel the posting. When Ojukwu learnt of what his father had done, he angrily resigned his job and drove all the way to Kaduna where he enlisted into the Nigerian Army as a lowly recruit.

The British officers at Kaduna kept wondering what an Oxford graduate was doing as a private in the Army and sent him for officers course in England. Ojukwu returned in 1957 and was commissioned a second Lieutenant, the first graduate to join the Nigerian Army.

Ojukwu rose rapidly through the Army. He was promoted to Lieutenant in 1958, Captain in 1960, Major in 1962 and Lieutenant Colonel in 1964.

Ojukwu was commander of the 4th battalion, Kano, when the first coup happened in January 1966.

As the coup unfolded, Major Nzeogwu called on Ojukwu to join the coup to which Ojukwu refused.

Ojukwus refusal to join Nzeogwu is one of the major reasons why Nzeogwu's coup eventually failed.

General Ironsi then seized power and appointed Ojukwu Military Governor of the Eastern Region.

6 months later, mid-level officers of the Nigerian of Northern extraction conducted a coup that led to the overthrow and killing of Ironsi, and the installment of Lt Col Yakubu Gowon as Head of State. The coup also greenlighted a pogrom in which over 30,000 Easterners,

mainly Igbos, were killed all over Nigeria, particularly in the North.

The inability of Gowon to stop the killings, the resentment in the Eastern Region against his government and the fact that Ojukwu was senior to Gowon caused bad blood between both men

The crisis became so bad that the then President of Ghana, General Joe Ankrah, intervened and invited both Gowon and Ojukwu to his Hilltop Mansion in Aburi, Ghana, for peace talks in January of 1967.

After two days of discussions, Ojukwu and Gowon signed an agreement that was to be known as the Aburi Accord.

A few months after their return from Ghana, Gowon broke the Aburi accord they signed by issuing decree 14 of 1967 which abolished all the 4 Regions, created 12 states, reversed the fiscal federalism practiced, changed the revenue sharing formula, all in a bid to increase the power of the North over the rest of Nigeria.

For Ojukwu, it was the last straw. Ojukwu convened the Eastern Nigerian Consultative Forum, a body that comprised of all the chiefs and head of the 20 provinces that made up the Eastern Region. They sat and discussed

for 2 days and mandated Ojukwu to declare the Eastern
Region a separate country. On the 30th of May 1967,
Ojukwu declared the Eastern Region a separate country
called the Republic of Biafra.

In retaliation, Gowon declared war. The war raged on for
3 years and ended in January 1970 with Ojukwu handing
over to his deputy, General Effiong, flying into exile in
Ivory Coast and the subsequent surrender of Biafra.

Ojukwu later returned from exile 12 years later. He died in
London in 2011 aged 78. His burial remains the greatest
ever witnessed in Nigeria.

Ojukwu is still revered by most old Eastern Nigeria
because we believe that he fought for our freedom.

The meaning of" Igbo kwenu "

what does "Igbo kwenu" mean? Why do none Igbo
culturally oriented and speaking peoples identify the Igbo
themselves with that phrasing "Igbo kwenu"? When the
Igbo say in a gathering "Igbo kwenu," what exactly are
they referring to or echoing out? Whose voice or voices
are embodied in the philosophy and culture of "Igbo
kwenu? Of what origin has the concept of "Igbo kwenu"?
Are there other societies known to the Igbo that share the

same collective wish to agree or disagree in a political or communal discourse of that nature? Why are the Igbo people sensitized with such an unshared cultural identity and representation?

To explain the cultural logic and symbolism of "Igbo kwenu" may not be as simple as it may look. I will therefore attempt and situate the concept of "Igbo kwenu" in the context of cultural identity, belongingness, solidarity and contribution to one's society.

The Phrase "Igbo Kwenu"

A common linguistic analysis may help us to understand the phrase "Igbo kwenu." Here we have two words: 'Igbo' and 'kwenu.' The term "Igbo" refers to Igbo people – men and women of all ages of tradition and modernism. On its own, "kwenu" as a word refers to agreement, endorsement, solidarity, unity, boundedness, strength, collective will.

The conception of the idea to stay together as a community and act as one is very important for the Igbo. The Igbo see the fact that to stay united in a direction or course of action will bring a shared honor to them. Therefore, they value strongly to come together. Coming together is deterministic and central to all else. In gathering of all sorts, namely marriage, rituals, celebrations, age grade meetings, war, wrestling, hunting, and village political affairs, the Igbo assert their emotions and psychology together through calls to order of solidarity such as invoking the "Igbo kwenu." Today, the Nigerian political class come up with all sorts of slogans not far from the culturally enhanced idiom of "Igbo kwenu." When someone is to speak to an issue, he will call to order the gathered Igbo to listen to him through the application or summon of "Igbo kwenu."

Traditionally, when a person among the gathered group intends to speak and has masterly and skillfully summoned attention with "Igbo kwenu," he is automatically granted audience. "Igbo kwenu" is a supreme call to attention and order to speak in a culturally appropriate way. Once the "Igbo kwenu" is announced and responded to, all ears will listen, at least momentarily to the person who surely will stand out and speak to them. His idea, point of information and facts, contribution and oratory skill will determine how much attention he will command. The Igbo can be noisy in public meeting sessions. Being noisy while discussing public affairs is not easily understood by the non-Igbo.

Speaking out loud and clear is a well cherished Igbo cultural feature. It is not merely seen or viewed as shouting or yelling, rather as a form of strength of communication and emphasis.

To trace the cultural origin of "Igbo kwenu" is a search for meaning and point of departure. It can be clearly said it is history of a culture in an unwritten form whose parts make up the whole. Like the history of the origin of the Igbo people of Nigeria, Igbo culture is attached to the shared meaning of Igbo life historically. There is no beginning and there is also no end in the dynamic relationship between ideology and realism. An inquiry into knowing and connecting the dots of the origin of the idiomatic notion of["Igbo kwenu" is hard to excavate and pin point to a specific historic and linguistic moment. Legends and creation myths told nothing to our common sense understanding about the first application of the phrase "Igbo kwenu." Yet important information gathered suggest that Igbo language, philosophy and manner of communication evolved as a collective praxis in charting their ways and transmission of life curiosities.

Some related stories asserted that the Igbo as a whole like to think and speak to and of things in a dynamic sense. There is an indication also of the fact that the Igbo reinvent any of their agreed upon matter of importance. As such, the "Igbo kwenu" concept captures there before, now and ahead of their time and events. Put practically, "Igbo kwenu" cuts short the form of saying - Igbo kwere na ihe ha kwuru (The Igbo believe in what they have agreed upon to think, say, and do). Classically, there is no record of history exclusive to the origin of the idiomatic connotation of "Igbo kwenu" this work came across in the search for knowing. Made to believe is that the phrase "Igbo kwenu" is aligned to Igbo language process on solidarity register and shared meaning of holding to what is agreed upon. We can deduce that "Igbo kwenu" is a psychic of a collective voice, the oratory skill and community action. Its origin and continuity have endured so much so that the significance of "Igbo kwenu" has become a norm in gathering of the Igbo for Igbo affairs.

A central way to explain the symbolism of "Igbo kwenu" is to refer to a local proverb which says: Ukwu diri otu, a kuo ulo gbam-gbam, ma ukwu adighi otu, a kuo ulo akirika (if we are united, we roof the house with a corrugated iron zinc; but, if we are not united, the house will be roofed with raffia palm). The proverb simplifies the obvious fact that unity is critical to any form of collective discourse, agreement, development action, connection and result. As when there is unity of purpose, the result of any action is comparable to roofing a house in a solid iron sheet. On the contrary, discourses that lack unity of minds and actions will result in disorder and of achieving less such that roofing a house is comparable to using vulnerable materials of less durability. The powerful proverb unveils the notion of ikwere or ekweghi.

(11)

THE OFO

The Ofo stick is passed down from father to 1st born son.

Ofo Nna endows the authority on the 1st born son as the leader & inheritor of the immediate patriarchal power of a nuclear lineage.

The Ofo Ndi Iche is the bigger Ofo which is handed to the Di Opara/Di Okpala/Di Okpa (Oldest surviving male son) of a larger descent group of the Umunna.

Along with other elders of the clan who are the leaders of each family (Onumara/Ezi/Ama) he regulates the authority of the particular clan.

The Ofo endows him with the authority of the ancestors. Each clan has such a man, and with other clan heads they govern the land as a council. When they gather, they do what is called, Iha Ofo (They line their ofo sticks on the ground according to the clan groupings).

In Igbo, "Ofo ha Otu" i.e. every Ofo is equal to the other, and collectively, they constitute the union of the people as a town. So, the ofo is a symbolic staff of authority.

(b) "Igo Ofo" is a ritual normally carried out on every Orie - the day of the ancestors; #Igbo day of rest and celebration of our ancestral links.

That day, every holder of the Ofo, makes offerings of wine & Kolanut to the great God Chineke and to the departed ancestral spirits of the land. They invoke God and the ancestors to make the land fruitful & equally prosperous for all; Banyere Nwoke, Banyere Nwanyi.

They ask for continuous fertility to help preserve and populate the land with children and with animals, which collectively are called; "Aku n'Uba".

They call for a balance in nature; "Ndu mmiri na Ndu Azu ".

They ask for forgiveness for any inadvertent infractions against the earth our mother, and the Great being at the realm beyond the skies.

Every man who has an Ofo must make these offerings we call "Igọ ọfọ" on this day in their own homesteads. This includes every male who has established his "Ihu Chi".

With the advent of Christianity, Igo Oji (Blessing of Kola nuts) is more widely practiced.

There are other types of Ofo such as; Ofo Nze and Ofo Dibia which compels 'native doctors' to adhere to Iwu Dibia (Code of Ethics).

(12)

OJUKWU WEPT

(A Leader Steeped in justice and Compassion)

This was an incident which taught me a big lesson. What happened was that there was a compromise between the Nigerian and Biafra troops; they decided to be friends and avoid killing each other. Their reason was that they reasoned that Ojukwu and Gowon were in bunkers, quite safe and they themselves were out there fighting, trying to kill one another. Why then should they be killing themselves? That was what we learnt later. So, they dug a massive hole, vowed, made a pledge that any arms supplied, they'd bury them there and get on with their friendship. It was sealed with parties.

They came over to the Biafra side to party and our people went to their side to party and our people supplied dancers, women, they supplied drinks and cigarettes and everything during the party. So, in one of the parties, our people suddenly took gun and arrested them; they said they were up to about 200. They then rented trucks and brought them to Umuahia and put them on parade. It was one of the rare incidences, which I remember, and it really struck me. They brought them in order to receive orders to execute them; that they were war prisoners. When we received them and lined them up, we went to tell Gen. Ojukwu the Biafra leader and he said it's impossible. He said "I'd investigate this, this is impossible. I'm a commander. As a military officer, I know that there's something in this." And he prepared and came and inspected the guard of honor. He went there but his fist was so tensed; after that he came out and began to cry and thundered;

"You thought I'm so bloodthirsty; you didn't execute them; you never executed them at the front, you brought them here for me to execute. Now take them away from here! camp them in your base and make sure you feed them till the end of the war."

That was highly emotional. Some of the people that were there can't remember. They would all have thought he would have said "take them away and execute them" but Ojukwu wouldn't do that. But the fact is that Nigerian soldiers, authorities and commanders could never believe or imagine that he could do this, because some of them were ruthless in their actions against our own people.

(13)

THE IGBO LANGUAGE WAR

The war against self is the worst of all wars. It is also the best of all wars. How you choose to war is solely up to you.' -MOB

The Igbo Language was recently accepted as an official language in Fox borough, Massachusetts, USA.

It became one of the major acknowledged languages alongside Yoruba and others.

It became officially stamped when the Department of Public Utilities adopted it and announced it in their memo.

This new development is ironic in that; while the West accommodates multiculturalism, here in Nigeria some ethnic people relegate local languages, including the Igbo.

We consider them tissue papers ready to flush down the cistern.

I could remember Onitsha and all the promises it holds for the great Igbo nation.

I grew up in that dense, non-sleepy town, and I like her for one thing, her peoples' undying love for culture.

When I refer to Onitsha, I meant it's indigenes, sons, and daughters of Ebo Itenani; Odoje, Ogbolieke, Umuaselle, Umudei, Mgbelekeke, Aroli, Umuaroli, Ogboli Olosi, Ogbotu, and Iyawu.

The descendants of Umuezechima.

I may dislike them for their jaundiced displeasing displacement of other Igbo groups who they often refer to as 'nwa onye Igbo' usually in a scathing sense of demeaning display of a king Kong chest or wave of the hand with an air of superiority, yet they hold the ace for the Igbo race.

Worse still they refer to all other Igbo, which is all non-Onitsha Igbo as 'Ndi-Igbo'.

I wonder then where they themselves came from, or what tribe group they belong to if they refer to others of the same stock as Ndi-Igbo.

Well, whether this was in part, one of the effects of the post-civil war of 1967-1970 is what I am yet to grasps.

Until I found out the origin, I rather remain as dumb as I am over the recklessness of those words.

On the opposite, in the entire vast Igbo space, Onitsha people seems to be the only Igbo group that very much upholds largely the sanctity of many of its own heritage, including its own variable Igbo dialect.

This isn't the first time I have commended Onitsha indigenous bravery and recommended that other Igbo groups should learn from them.

I have been privy to the inner workings of many Onitsha family, and I can say that Christianity has its place just like tradition.

They give attention to both soundly and have shown pleasure and pride in every sense of it.

They are early runners of the Christian religion in southeast Nigeria, earlier than any other town, and so they are Anglican or Catholic, with a sprinkle of Pentecostals summed up in a popular our Savior's Church, a fusion of the two above founded by Late Justice Chuba Ikpeazu.

In addition, I have witnessed many times, the coming home of many Onitsha families from Europe and the US, and each time I am amazed at how their kids spoke Onitsha dialectic fluently.

And more so how for a good number of times returnees take Ozo title with their kids before heading back to their base.

It is unbelievable.

It is also unbelievable how someone who lives far away, in the terraces of London, at a basement in New York and at a penthouse in Paris would speak Igbo with a local accent, while someone who lives in Awada Onitsha, Umuokpu

Awka, or in Uruagu Nnewi would seemingly be proud to the deficiency of Igbo speaking demonstrated by his or her kids despite living within the space where the language is openly and freely spoken.

Ridiculous.

The systemic and deliberate attempt to handicap the Igbo children of tomorrow has started in earnest that schools, notoriously private schools have sowed the seed of Igbo language deletion from the consciousness of the pupils and students.

I was appalled when I visited the house of a family at Nkpor by Old road, only to found out that his kids, one; 12 years and the other 9 years know nothing of Igbo.

They do not speak, although they could hear at least the basic words.

I could see how proud their father was; pride in his son's apparent handicap.

And like I said they live at Nkpor.

I mean Nkpor Uno.

Chimamanda Adichie does not have a grasp of Igbo so well, and to her, it isn't great.

She sees it as a handicap and wished she knows how to speak.

I consider it unfair that a parent could speak Igbo language but would fail to provide such privilege for their growing kids.

Though I am certain that these languages will fade away to the wide and influential English, one to be spoken by a very little number of people, it isn't anywhere near.

It is a duty of an Igbo parent to understand that multicultural society isn't yet dead and until then, we must teach children Igbo.

This is a war within, how we choose to war is up to us.

(14)

THE WHITE MAN ON A BIKE

(a stop and gossip on the road from Owerrinta to Owerri)

The story of a white man dragged off a bicycle and killed while riding in the Igbo country has been told in different ways, even in Chinua Achebe's "Things Fall Apart". The man, a doctor named Stewart, was actually killed due to mistaken identity during resistance to the British.

The incident happened in November 1905, in Mbaise, while Dr. Stewart was attempting to catch up with a convoy of colonial troops from Owere to Calabar by bicycle. He was captured and paraded through several areas and finally killed in the Afo market of Onicha Amairi, his body never found.

Stewart was actually mistaken for a man named Harold M. Douglas, the first District Commissioner of the new colonial Owerri District, who is noted in oral tradition and official colonial reports for his ruthlessness.

H. M. Douglas was noted for his focus on building roads which were built with forced labor gotten through Warrant Chiefs and the prisons. Douglas' reputation for abuse and the colonial imposition in general led to the intense hostility towards Europeans in the Owere area.

The killing of Dr. Stewart was blamed on the Ahiara which led to the punitive Ahiara Expedition of December 1905 in which many lives and properties in the Ahiara area were lost. Whole villages were levelled and many were taken as prisoners.

Douglas Road, the main road through Owere town, was named after the brutal H. M. Douglas, so was Douglas House, the main seat of what is now the Imo State government.

Under the colonial regime, roads, and later the railway, were built with forced labor. Prisoners were also used as slave labor and were also loaned out for private uses. Africans were sent to prison for minor offences to provide prison labor.

The British administration in the southeastern area was inefficient and inconsistent. There was a prevalence of violence and corruption.

Untrained colonial officers found themselves in isolated areas where many took advantage of the lack of supervision and the permission to use force and violence to quell the sporadic resistances to British imperialism in the area.

Violence became a persuasive tool that permeated all levels of the colonial administration, including through the 'native' warrant chiefs. Despite this, resistance lasted roughly from the 1880s and well into the 1920s.

Moral of the story: The Igbo man hated oppression and still does. Don't ask him to stop fighting, he will never stop.

(15)

IGBO ALPHABETS AND THE SPELLING.

A B CH D E F G GB GH GW H I Ị J K KP KW L M N Ñ NW NY O

Ọ P R S SH T U Ụ V W Y Z.

8 Vowels (Ụdaume)

28 Consonants (Mgbochiume)

36 Alphabets (Mkpụrụedemede/Abidii).

(16)

SOME IGBO WORDS AND ENGLISH MEANINGS

Ugegbe - Mirror

Ihe Onyonyo - TV

Mister - Mazi

Ajadu or isi nkpe - Widow

Usekwu - Kitchen

Cat - Nwamba

Ide Mmiri - Flood

Oriọna - Lamp

Mahadum - University

Certificate - Asambodo

AC/Fan - Ntụ oyi

Prison - Ụlọ Mkpọrọ

Orphan - Nwa mgbei

Bottle - Kalama/Ekpem

Diviner - Ọgba afa

Midnight - Ndeli

Train- Ụgbọ oloko

Phone- Ekwentị

Library - Ọba Akwụkwọ

Neighbor - Agbataobi

Tapioca- Abacha

1,000 - Otu Puku

2,000 – puku abuo

100 – otu naari

200 – naari abuo

10 – iri

20 – iri abuo

Professor- Ọkammụta

Etc - Ya dịrị gabazia (ydgz).

ACKNOWLEDGEMENT

with a heart full of gratitude, I wish to appreciate my sweet and beloved step mother **Tamara voorn** for her love and selfless supports and encouragements, she's always been a role model and inspiration to me.

Not forgetting also my step sister **Soraya**, who in many ways unknown to her, have been an inspiration to me. Another person is my beloved mother **Mrs. blessing ezeribe**, for her love and support towards us her children, my beloved siblings and entire family, am so grateful for all you've done for me, may you all be blessed beyond measures.